HARLAND & WOLFF
AND
WORKMAN, CLARK

HARLAND & WOLFF

AND

WORKMAN, CLARK

A GOLDEN AGE OF SHIPBUILDING IN OLD IMAGES

RICHARD P. DE KERBRECH AND DAVID L. WILLIAMS

The
History
Press

Frotn cover: Launch of the *Titanic* on 31 May 1911. (From the Kempster album, courtesy of Steve Raffield)

Back cover: The *Titanic* in dry dock at Belfast in early February 1912, to have her propellers fitted. On the pontoon beneath the crane is the solid cast centre propeller.(Authors' collection)

Frontispiece: Photo of Bibby Lines SS *Oxfordshire* (Yard No. 429) dressed fully overall in the River Mersey in preparation for her maiden voyage on 17 September 1912. She was engined with the cumbersome quadruple-expansion steam machinery. (B. & A. Feilden)

Right: An advert that appeared in a publicity book published by Workman, Clark for The Globe Pneumatic Engineering Company which specialised in pneumatic riveters, caulkers, drills, scalers and chippers, as used in the Workman, Clark yard. (Courtesy Dr John Lynch)

First published 2021

The History Press
97 St George's Place, Cheltenham,
Gloucestershire, GL50 3QB
www.thehistorypress.co.uk

British Library Cataloguing in Publication Data.
A catalogue record for this book is available from the British Library.

ISBN 978 0 7509 9734 8

Typesetting and origination by The History Press
Printed in Turkey by Imak

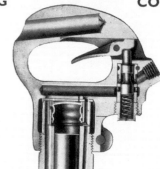

CONTENTS

Newspaper report from c.1897. Launch of an Atlantic liner plus view of Framing and Plating shed. (Authors' collection)

LAUNCHING AN ATLANTIC LINER AT MESSRS. HARLAND AND WOLFF'S, BELFAST.

FRAMING AND PLATING SHEDS, SHOWING MACHINERY FOR DRILLING HOLES IN STEEL PLATES FOR SHIPBUILDING.

The works of Messrs. Harland and Wolff, which, some forty years ago covered two or three acres, and employed a couple of hundred men, now cover nearly eighty acres, and pay wages amounting to £12,000 to £14,000 per week. The tonnage of the vessels built during 1896 amounted to 81,000 tons, considerably more than the output of all the five Government yards.

INTRODUCTION

A ship – designed by geniuses, built by skilled craftsmen and manned by idiots.

Photo of Harland & Wolff Yard in 1884 with ships at fitting-out jetties at Queen's Island. Note the four-masted barque between the steamers with the helm (wheel) and the counter stern that housed the tiller. Also, the plate rudder, the hallmark of some of Harland's later ships. (Authors' collection)

The *German* (Yard No. 334), a small vessel launched on 4 August 1898 from No. 9 slipway in the South Yard, was completed in November 1898 for the Union Steamship Company. A good view between her twin triple expansion steam engines looking towards the manoeuvring platform. She survived until 1930 when she was broken up. (Alan Mallett collection)

The *Galeka* (Yard No. 347). A sister of Union Steamship Company's *German*, she is seen here on 21 October 1899 in a stationary stern view ready for launching from No. 9 slipway in the South Yard. On 26 October 1916 she struck a mine at the entrance to Le Havre as HMHS *Galeka* and sank with a loss of nineteen lives. (Alan Mallett collection)

Some of the more famous industries in Belfast's past include the shipbuilders Harland & Wolff and Workman, Clark; aircraft builders Short Brothers, later Short and Harland; Sirocco Fans; Linen, Belfast was known at one time as 'Linenopolis'; De Lorean cars; as well as rope makers and breweries.

So why Harland & Wolff and Workman, Clark? The former was well documented by professional photographer Robert Welch (1859–1936) who was the shipyard's photographer from 1894–1920.

It is hard to define 'A Golden Age' but the authors have tried to give this work a snapshot of an era. For a start, this work is not a description, guide or history of the yards, nor is it a treatise or monograph on shipbuilding or shipyard practice. It is a random selection of old, mainly late Victorian, Edwardian and 1920s images of shipbuilding and engineering craftsmen at work. Some images are outside this timescale and although they are chiefly of the Harland & Wolff and Workman, Clark yards, some have been gleaned from British shipyards elsewhere. These have been captioned appropriately to describe certain trades. As can be expected on a work about shipbuilding, there are plenty of photographs of ships being launched. The emphasis is on passenger ships built by both companies during peacetime.

Although wooden shipbuilding on the banks of the River Lagan had started with a regular supply of timber, by the time steel shipbuilding had been established there was no indigenous iron ore or coal in Ireland to supply the industry. As Harland & Wolff progressed from wood to iron to steel, all forms of supply, like iron and steel in the form of steel girders, plates, angle iron, 'I' section beams, pig iron and sand for casting, coal and coke for forges, had to be imported to Belfast. Steel was supplied by The Darlington Steel & Iron Company and the 'spectacle' brackets that housed the propeller shafts, the rudder and its mounting were supplied by the Darlington Forge Company, both in the North-East of England. Timber was supplied by Irvin & Sellars, and James P. Corry. All machine tools like lathes, milling machines, pillar drills, and boring machines were manufactured in the UK.

Harland & Wolff survived two world wars, including the Blitz of 7–8 and 15 April 1941; Partition – Home Rule for Ireland; the Irish Civil War; The Depression; 'The Troubles'; British Shipbuilders, only to cease trading on 5 August 2019.

Internal strife for the workforce throughout the years were fear of Home Rule for Ireland, rampant trade unionism and disputes, sectarianism and threats by the IRA, quite apart from spartan working conditions and poor wages.

In order to focus on the main topic, distractions such as sectarianism, employment/non-employment of Catholics, Irish Home Rule and Membership of the Orange Order, which might prove contentious, have been avoided.

It is hard to imagine the sheer cacophony of noise generated when a ship is being built. The relentless sound of riveting hammers, pneumatic riveters, pneumatic caulking hammers, drills, flogging hammers, metal bashing and men shouting which could be heard way across the city. The sheer danger of the hazards from pneumatic hoses, lead lamp cables, oxy-acetylene cylinders and hoses strewn across the deck; access holes and openings uncovered. Pipes being fitted with gangs of pipefitters mooching about with lengths of piping over their shoulders, then turning, oblivious to any personnel at close quarters who had to duck in time. Below decks, electricians running miles of electric cabling via wire cable nests, wires hanging down before being tidied and secured.

Heavy steel plates being lifted by overhead cranes to be located and bolted to the requisite frames prior to riveting. Heavy components overhead traversing the structure by crane. And sometimes tools being (accidentally) dropped from a great height. No wonder the yard foremen wore reinforced bowler hats for protection as well as for recognition and authority. As the ship's structure grew and took on an enclosed box-like building, so the noise was further resonated and amplified. Wet and windy weather added extra dangers to those working out on the slipways. Working outside in very cold weather was also a hazardous environment.

Although not so dangerous, there were those characteristic shipyard smells in the workshops; the smell of mineral oil, sperm oil and soluble oil used as 'slurry' or cutting oil, tallow, tar, oakum, red lead paint and paraffin in the brass shop. The smell of leather from the plethora of belt drives. In the foundry the pungent smell of sulphur when the molten metal had burned the casting sand adjacent to it. The smell of coke from the smithy and the individual rivet braziers. In the joiners' and wood finishing shops the aroma of freshly cut wood such as cedar, oak, pine and teak as well as linseed oil, beeswax and French polishing. Personal smells like pipe tobacco and cigarettes being smoked as well as body odour. (In this era, baths were rare in workers' houses; baths were either galvanised tubs stored in the back yard or a visit to the Public Baths. Bath time was generally once a week, and a change into fresh underclothes, in a time before deodorants.)

Turning a main crankshaft journal in the lathe in the Engine Works for the engines of White Star's *Oceanic* (II), (Yard No. 317) on 1 October 1898. When complete, the two sets of engines were the largest in the world. Note the huge counterbalance weights on the chuck, the large circular plate that secures the shaft. This task was a most exacting and prestigious turning job performed by a top-class tradesman. The lathe itself was made by Thomas Shanks & Co. of Johnstone, near Paisley, a former venerable Scottish manufacturer of machine tools. (Authors' collection)

LAUNCH OF A VESSEL AT BELFAST

The launch of the *Oceanic* (II) at Belfast on 14 January 1899 from No. 2 slipway in the North Yard. Note the propellers already fitted, turning as they enter the water. The blurred part that appears on the ship's port side may be a drag chain taking up the tension in order to slow down the vessel's momentum during the launching. (Authors' collection)

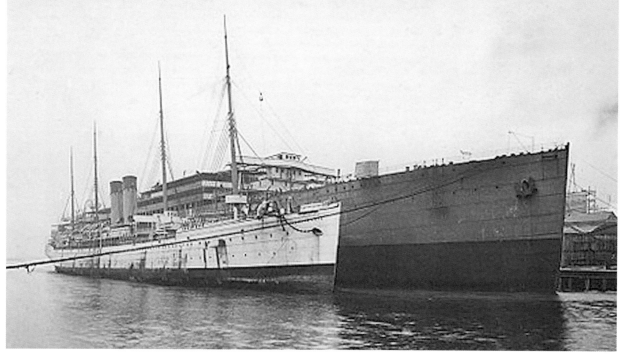

The starboard bow view of White Star's *Cedric* (Yard No. 337) fitting out alongside the Alexandra Berth with the *Britannic* (I) of 1874 (Yard No. 83) moored alongside, during September 1902. The *Britannic* had completed trooping duties to South Africa for the Boer War before being sold the following year. This photo probably best represents the 'nursery and the knackers yard'. (Authors' collection)

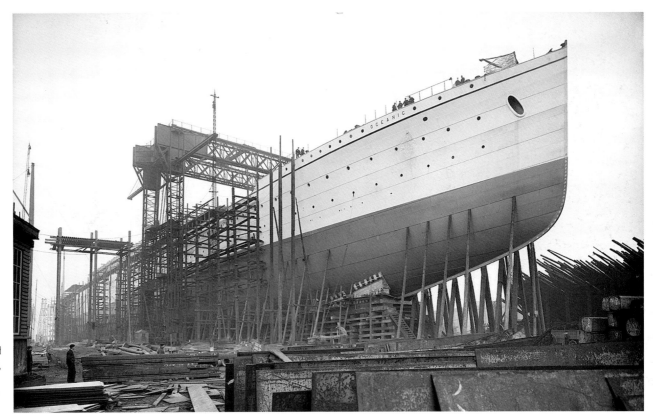

The *Oceanic* (II), showing starboard bow three-quarter profile on the slip prior to launch, with topside painted light grey. The shoring and the forward part of the cradle, the forward poppet, are clearly in view. In the surrounding yard may be seen stock steel plate for future construction. (Robert Welch)

All of this took place in an era of total industrialisation, in a time before the Factories Act of 1937, the Health & Safety Act of 1974, computerisation, digitisation and globalisation. Safe working practices were mainly observed by common sense and potential dangers alerted by wise council from one's more experienced artisans.

Shipyard practices and factory codes were much the same throughout Britain, on the River Clyde, the River Mersey and the Tyne, Wear and Tees. Although the trades did the same nature of work, wage differentials existed throughout the land.

Many of the images show work being done on ships of the White Star Line and other shipping company passenger ships, and there is also a slant towards the 'Olympic'-class liners, the *Olympic*, *Titanic* and *Britannic*, the largest liners, along with Cunard's Clyde-built *Aquitania*, ever built in the British Isles up until the advent of the *Queen Mary* of 1936.

One of Harland & Wolff's specialisms was the power plant of large ships propelled by three propellers. This involved the installation of what was then known as 'combination machinery', whereby the two wing propellers were driven by high-power steam reciprocating engines, the exhaust steam of which was directed through a large Low Pressure Parsons steam turbine driving a central propeller. Some twenty-two of Harland & Wolff's ships were fitted with this power plant.

The working week for the main blue-collar workforce started at 6.30 a.m. when they clocked on. The 'knock off' whistle ended their day at 5.30 p.m. On Saturdays, the day started at 6.30 a.m. until 1.30 p.m. Meal breaks were allowed during weekdays between 8.20 a.m. and 9.00 a.m. and from 1.00 p.m. to 2.00 p.m. Only a breakfast break was allowed on Saturdays, making the working week around sixty hours in total. They ate, not in the firm's dining rooms enjoyed by the shipyard's management, but at their workstations in the shops or in the shadows of the ships being built. They supplied their own food for the meals. Average weekly wages for a boilermaker would be around £2.2*s* (£2.10) and for other tradesmen around £1.10*s*–£1.15*s* (£1.50–£1.75).

Above: The *Adriatic* (II) (Yard No. 358) being made ready for launching on slipway No. 3 at Harland & Wolff's North Yard on 20 September 1906. Her drag anchors are rigged in readiness and the fore poppet of her cradle has been constructed. (Real Photographs Co. Ltd)

Left: Union-Castle Line's *Dunluce Castle* (II) (Yard No. 361) following her launch on 31 March 1904 from No. 7 slipway in the South Yard. (Alan Mallett collection)

ABBREVIATIONS

psi	pounds per square inch (lb/in²)
rev/min	revolutions per minute
mv	motor vessel
ihp	Indicated Horsepower (steam reciprocating engines)
shp	Shaft Horsepower (steam turbines)
bhp	Brake Horsepower (diesel engines)
NMNI	National Museums of Northern Ireland
UF&TM	Ulster Folk & Transport Museum

Note: In the text some ships' names have a Roman numeral in brackets after them, e.g. *Britannic* (II). This indicates that it is a second ship of the name built for a company.

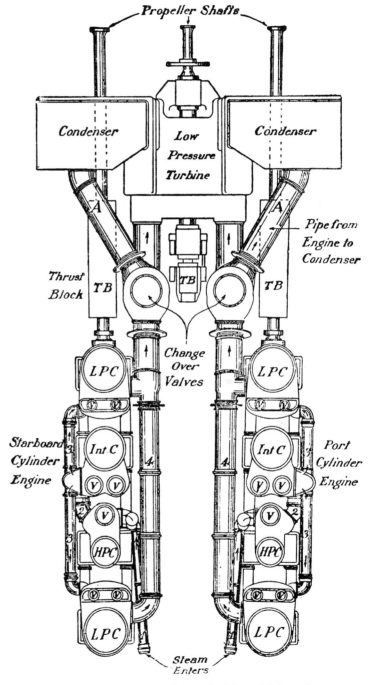

Schematic layout of a typical combination machinery. (Authors' collection)

Triple expansion engines and exhaust turbine, driving three screws.

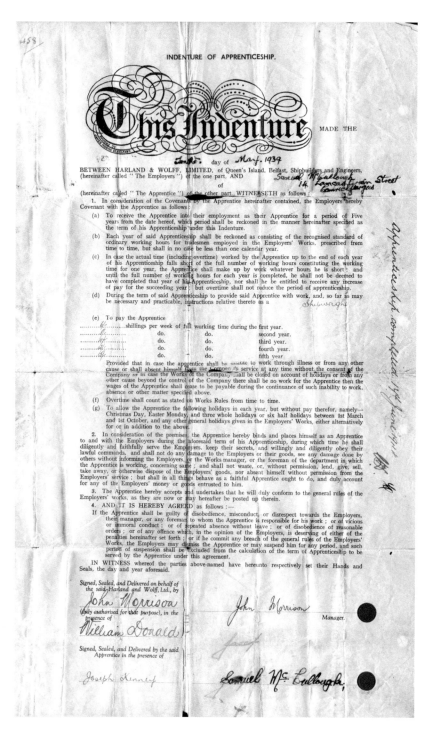

Above: Hydraulic Riveting on the *Olympic*'s keel (Yard No. 400). This horseshoe-shaped calliper could exert a pressure of 40–55 psi when operated. It is suspended from a moving crane on top of the gantry. The hoses to the left are supplying hydraulic fluid to the machine, and to the right are the rivet gang with the brazier heating the rivets. (NMNI)

Left: Harland & Wolff Apprenticeship Indenture of Samuel McCullough, a Shipwright who commenced his apprenticeship on 10 May 1939 and completed it on 17 June 1944. (Authors' collection)

I. SHIPYARD TRADES

Never call a Joiner a Carpenter or a Cabinet-maker a Joiner and never call any of them a Shipwright.
Always refer to a carpenter as 'Chippie'.

Depending on one's background, not everyone was successful in obtaining an apprenticeship or other employment at Harland & Wolff.

SHIPYARD TRADES

Trades engaged in the Shipyard

Blacksmiths	Patternmakers
Blacksmiths Strikers	Platers & Helpers
Blacksmiths Helpers	Plumbers
Boatbuilders	Polishers
Boilermakers	Red leaders
Brassmoulders	Riggers & Helpers
Cabinetmakers	Rivet Counters
Caulkers	Riveters (Heater Boy, Catch
Coppersmiths	Boy & Holder-up)
Crane Drivers	Sawers
Drillers	Sheetmetal workers
Electricians	Shipwrights
Fitters	Stablemen
Hole Cutters	Stagers
Ironmen	Storemen
Iron Sorters	Tinsmith
Joiners	Turners
Joiners in ships	Woodturners
Labourers	Works Firemen (with fire
Loftsmen Minute men	engine)
Painters	

Trades engaged in the Offices

Accountants	Naval Architects
Bookkeepers	Secretaries
Cooks and ancillary staff	Tracers
Cleaners	Telephonists
Draughtsmen	Time keepers
Message Boys	Managers

Above and left: Shipyard Trades in Edwardian times. Note the absence of welders as this method of fastening of plates had not been perfected as a replacement to riveting. (Stephen Cameron)

In Victorian and Edwardian times, and indeed up until the 1970s, shipyard trades were many and demarcation was the order of the day. A list of shipyard trades shows the legion of different trades. In turn, each trade could be stratified into skilled, semi-skilled and unskilled. One could progress to being a skilled craftsman from apprentice to journeyman, skilled craftsman, and sometimes to the antiquated title of master craftsman. A look at the list shows that some trades are self-explanatory while others may require some further description. Yards such as Harland & Wolff and Workman, Clark would employ legions of apprentices in various stages of their five-year apprenticeship at the time. There was probably a ratio of ten journeymen to one apprentice. Although learning a trade, this was also a very good source of cheap labour. This five-year apprenticeship had been reduced from seven years early in the twentieth century, although some boys joined the yards at 14 but completion of an apprenticeship was always on or near their 21st birthday.

Concerning the various trades, riveters, along with caulkers, platers, blacksmiths, angle-iron smiths, sheet iron workers, coppersmiths, shipwrights, loftsmen and burners comprised the 'black squad', the workers who actually put together the structure of a vessel. Then there were the finishing trades like plumbers, engineers, electricians, joiners, carpenters, riggers, upholsterers and painters. In the engine shops there were turners, fitters, engineers and brass finishers.

In the boiler shop there were platers, riveters, pressers, and boilermakers. It is worth having a look at some of these trades in a bit more in detail.

The blacksmith, one of the oldest trades, was the tradesman who worked red-hot steel and iron to various shapes. He would be the leader of a team, which comprised a 'striker' who delivered hammer blows to hot metal on the anvil which the blacksmith would rotate and fashion it to the required shape. His other helper would ensure the coke in the forge was replenished and kept red hot and also tend to the bellows. Later, during the introduction of the steam-operated hammer, the striker was replaced.

Frame-bending. These men, probably angle-iron smiths or ironmen, are bending a red-hot frame, with the help of a hydraulically-operated bending tool. Note the foreman on the far right with the bowler hat overseeing the team who wear flat caps or 'dunchers'. Foremen at the yard were known as 'hats'. (Authors' collection)

The *Titanic* (Yard No. 401), under construction to 'C' Deck. Note the riveters at the distant right-hand side of the casing opening and the 'holder-up' on the deck beneath. (David Hutchings collection)

Riveting was another trade that required more than one operative to perform the task. A fully detailed account of this process is given in Stephen Cameron's book *Belfast Shipbuilders – A Titanic Tale*:

Considered by most to be the 'Kings of the workforce' were the riveters. Each gang consisted of five people. In charge of the squad was the right-handed riveter, who along with a left-handed riveter would between them hammer the head onto the hot rivet. They would work as a pair and once a successful pairing was established it would normally last for years. Obviously there were thousands and thousands of rivets that would need to be put in place in the construction of a ship. Ensuring that a steady supply of near yellow-hot rivets was continually provided for the two riveters was the role of the three other members of the gang, a heater boy, a catch boy and a holder-up. For the whole system to work smoothly teamwork was needed.

Hand riveters at work near the bow of the *Britannic* (II) (Yard No. 433). The seeming lack of activity, apart from this group, indicates that this photograph may have been posed. Hand riveting was carried out where the hydraulic riveting machine could not reach. Some 3 million rivets were used in the construction of the *Titanic*'s hull, one-third of which were fastened with a hydraulic riveter. (Authors' collection)

The heater boy was generally a very young and unskilled boy (although the term 'boy' applied to the job and not the person, and many men were still rivet boys at retirement) in charge of the brazier that heated the rivets. His job was to maintain a steady supply of correctly heated rivets. His initial training amounted to him being shown how to keep the brazier well stoked, how to ensure a continuous supply of rivets being placed in the brazier and then, finally, watching the rivets heat to the correct temperature as determined by its colour. The squad's pay was based on the number of rivets that they drove home; the more rivets in place, the larger the pay out at the end of the week. Around the time of the construction of the 'Olympic'-class ships, in the early 1900s, the riveters were being paid one old half penny per rivet that was hammered home. This meant that they had to put in 480 rivets to earn £1. This was then divided between them. With this in mind, it was of the utmost importance that the squad could start working as soon as possible from the beginning of each shift. This meant that the heater boy had to 'break into' the yard before starting time in the morning and get the brazier lit, and have it up to working temperature as early as possible, thereby ensuring that the squad could be at work as soon as possible. Meal breaks were also the time for him to tend to the brazier and ensure he had sufficient coke to fuel the fire.

Above: This photo was taken at a shipyard on the River Clyde in April 1918. In the foreground may be seen the braziers heating the rivets minded by the rivet 'boys'. To right in the background may be seen some female workers, as they would have augmented the workforce when many shipyard workers were conscripted. The same would have been the case at Harland & Wolff, with women brought in to supplement the labour shortage. They were called 'dilutees' and proved themselves competent in their allotted tasks. (World Ship Society)

Right: This little chap is a very young heater boy at the rivet brazier in the J. L. Thompson's Shipyard in Sunderland. He is pumping the bellows with his right foot in order to maintain the brazier coke at high temperature. (Tyne & Wear Archives & Museums)

Man operating a boring machine, boring out a hollow shaft at John I. Thornycroft's yard at Southampton. The shaft is secured in this machine and the tool rotated on a fly-cutter and fed into the shaft from the left. (David Hutchings collection)

Once the rivet was heated to the correct colour (for steel up to bright yellow, for iron rivets to almost a white heat), the heater boy would take it out of the brazier with a large pair of tongs and give it to the catch boy, also a young lad. Depending on how or where in the ship they were working, the heater boy would either slide the yellow-hot rivet along a metal plate to the catch boy or throw it to him. The catch boy could catch it in a large asbestos mitt (or maybe a small bucket) and then quickly throw it to the holder-up, who would catch it in a large tin and with a pair of tongs swiftly transfer it to the lined up holes in the plates that were being joined together. The catch boy would only ever be issued with one mitt. Once it wore out he would either have to make a leather patch and tie it to his hand, or else do without. This method would result in his hand becoming burnt very quickly and would callous over as he caught and threw on the hot rivet. Once inserted in place, the holder-up (or holder-on), again a young lad, would use a wooden cradle, known as a 'dolly', against his shoulder to brace the rivet. On the other side of the plates the two riveters would start hammering at the rivet and shape the head on it in less than a minute. They would then quickly progress to the next rivet that the holder-up would push through from the underside. From the minute the rivet was taken out of the brazier it started to cool down, so it was vitally important that the rivet was speedily delivered to the riveters before it cooled to such a temperature that it was no longer malleable enough to have the head worked on it.

Following after the squad were the unpopular rivet counters. Their job was twofold: firstly, to check that an acceptable standard of riveting was being met; and also to count the number of rivets being put in. It was on this number that the wages of the entire squad would be based. If the riveting was below standard, the counter would draw a chalk circle around the faulty rivet and the squad, at their own expense, would have to have this rivet drilled out and then re-riveted.

Hand riveting was later replaced with pneumatic and hydraulic riveting, which took away the need for the right- and left-handed riveters. The device, a large horseshoe calliper-shaped machine, would be suspended by a crane over the area to be riveted. At each end of the arms of the machine were two rams that on the operation of a lever would close tightly under hydraulic pressure. The yellow-hot rivet would be put into the required hole, the riveter would line up the rams which had metal cups at their ends. These cups would hold the rivet in place while the rams were pushed together, compressing the rivet. Once that was done the riveter would increase the pressure in the machine

to full power and the cups, under enormous hydraulic pressure, would close tightly and in doing so would then form the head of the hot rivet. This method was quicker than hand riveting, and when it was finished the rivet would be red-hot by this time and contracting, which would make it pull the plates together and make a tighter joint in the plates. This hydraulic system, while faster, could not be carried out in confined spaces, so there was always a need for the hand riveters.

The squad had to work very closely with each other. If one of the 'paired' hand riveters didn't turn up for work, it would have been very difficult for the other riveter to work with anyone else, as they worked in tandem. Communication between the squad was difficult due to the incessant noise that was created by all the riveting squads throughout the yard. Normally they used a form of code by tapping on the hull to tell those on the other side what they wanted. Deafness was a major problem for these men, as they were subjected to continuous loud noise without any form of ear protection, but back in those days if one became deaf because of the nature of work, people would shout at them to be heard. The preferred clothing of riveters was generally dark moleskin trousers with straps around the knees.

Above left: The centre keel plate of the *Aquitania* being laid down at John Brown on Clydebank. Note that the keel plate lies on the blocks which had to be at least 6ft high for the workmen to pass underneath. What is actually in view is one side of the box keel. (Authors' collection)

Above right: These men are hydraulically riveting plates to the side of the *Aquitania* being built on Clydebank. (Authors' collection)

The hole cutter. By means of a pneumatically driven throttle, round sidelights/portholes are cut into the ship's hull. This method operated similar to a modern trepanning tool, the small cog on his hand-held throttle engages with the large gearwheel. (Authors' collection)

Another photo of the hole cutter showing more progress on this process, when cut through the large cut steel disc will fall outwards onto the scaffolding by the operator. (Authors' collection)

Closely allied to the rivet squad were the caulkers, whose pneumatic chisel-edged tool crimped the plates after riveting to ensure water-tightness. The trade had evolved from iron-ship caulkers to steel-built vessels.

In the pubs in Belfast on pay days, riveters and caulkers could be identified if they lined the bar as they were the clientele that didn't turn around to see who came into the pub after the public bar door latch sounded, as they didn't hear it!

Another highly skilled craft was that of the boilermaker. Like the shipbuilding rivet squad, they were also specialist riveters with the same tasks, only they worked in the comfort of the enclosed Boiler Shop instead of outside on the exposed slipways.

In the manufacture of cylindrical fire tube or Scotch boilers, plate had to be rolled between large rollers to produce its curved profile prior to assembly. When cylindrical boiler shells were being brought together and the end covers riveted in place, often the holder-up would be on the inside and the riveters or pneumatic riveter working from the exterior to shape the head. The noise inside the boiler would have been loud and deafening. On completion of the work inside the boilers, the holder-up would exit via the manhole apertures. The construction of these huge pressure vessels required great skill, for apart from riveting the seams, fire tubes and stays had to be fitted into the boiler. Boilers had to be water, steam and pressure tight, as well as being able to withstand high steam temperatures and furnace temperatures up to 2,600°F. Unlike the plates of the ships' hulls, boiler riveted seams were not caulked. In addition, their union, the United Society of Boilermakers & Iron & Steel Shipbuilders, formed as far back as 1834, was active in protecting its members. The Union always admitted boilermakers, platers, riveters, holders-up, caulkers and anglesmiths. By 1912 it admitted draughtsmen working on shipbuilding and iron and steel construction.

The shipwrights belonged to one of the oldest trades in the world. The definition of a shipwright according to Captain Paasch's *Illustrated Marine Encyclopaedia 1890*:

A ship-builder; but the term more properly applies to the skilled artisan, who performs the practical part of the work. Viz: The putting together and fastening the various parts of a vessel shaped in accordance with the designs of a Naval Architect. Name also given to one engaged in caulking and remetalling of wooden vessels, renewing or repairing of decks, in-, or outside planking, etc., for which the art of a designer is not required.

The Thor pneumatic riveting hammer. The holder-up to the left is bracing the rivet in place with a tool called a 'dolly' which cannot be seen in this photo. The riveter is operating in the down hand mode. This machine mimicked continuous hammering. Judging by the shape of the gunwale they are on the stern of a tug or tender in a small shipyard. (Authors' collection)

The Thor pneumatic drill. This photo shows a driller at work, and shows the utility of the drill when working in a corner. (Authors' collection)

Although essentially accurate, perhaps the definition was a little generic by Edwardian standards of the day, for when ships were constructed of wood and sail, the shipwright played a much more important and central part when he was the supreme builder responsible for all aspects of the basic construction. Also, in these early days the Master Shipwright was the top post in the Royal Dockyards. In later years, the shipwright was hemmed in by the metal tradesmen such as the platers or the joiners responsible for fitting out work, so reluctantly they initially made the transition from wood to being iron shipwrights.

By the time of the late Victorian and early Edwardian era, their duties were more clearly defined, as by 1882 they had established their own trade union, the Shipconstructors' & Shipwrights' Association. They could work between metal and wood, as such they were first involved in setting up the keel blocks on which the keel of a new vessel was laid on the concrete building berth or slipway. These blocks were set in a line and comprised large oak baulks chocked with strategically-placed wedges and topped by a crown a little over 6 feet high. The shipwrights' preferred rig was a monkey-jacket and the top button had to be of brass.

The shipwrights, along with the platers, had the task of preparing, erecting and fairing the frames and plates that were to be riveted together.

As the frames and plates of the outer hull spread outwards from the keel they were shored up with timber props like short telegraph poles, referred to as shores. As the ship grew, the shipwrights constructed the ground ways as part of the cradle down which the ship would glide into the water. These were built equidistant from the keel. At the bow and stern, the forward and after 'poppets' were constructed to support the ship on the sliding ways and the bow as it pivoted as the stern entered the water. (Poppet: the wooden structures made up of saddles and braces built up at the bow and stern of ship; these were adjusted by wedges and packing.)

Prior to any launching, the shipwrights commenced the labour-intensive tasks of greasing the ground ways. Wedges were then manually driven up, which brought the poppets and packing hard up against the ship's hull. The shores were removed from between the ways and the wedges were again driven up. The removal of the keel blocks and the remaining shores took place simultaneously. When these were removed, the vessel was resting on the launching cradle and was ready for its release during the launching ceremony.

A labour-intensive task with an army of shipwrights setting up the after poppet of a large warship in preparation for launching. They are swinging their 'mauls' on both sides of the cradle. (Crown copyright)

Shipwrights would then be involved during the fitting-out of the ship by building doors, frames and wall panelling. The teak decking was laid and bolted to the steel deck, the holes where the fastenings were made were plugged and the decking caulked. Shipwrights could also be switched to boatbuilding alongside time-served boat builders that built ships' lifeboats.

Another specialised woodworking trade was the patternmaker, who made the detailed wooden patterns for items to be cast, both large and small. The patterns would be used over and over again, where the shape was used when sand moulds were compacted around it, then it was removed before molten metal was poured into the cavity. Depending on which material was being cast, iron, steel, brass or bronze, the patternmaker would make the pattern incrementally, dimensionally oversize to compensate for the molten metal shrinking during solidification.

Woodworking trades had their own social stratification. At the top of the tree, so to speak, were the cabinetmakers who built the full-size mock-up of the cabins and public rooms as an example of that which would be fitted into the ship. All intricate and top class furniture was made by them to be fitted on board, along with the intricate oak panelling and decorative carved mouldings, including cherubs.

Cabinet makers working on the mouldings of the *Olympic*. (Harland & Wolff)

In the past there had been disputes between shipwrights and joiners over demarcation, but by the turn of the century this had been resolved.

The joiners and joiners-in-ships also made furniture and stairway banisters and fitted out the cabins, as they had done in the days of wooden shipbuilding. They could sometimes be recognised as many liked to wear a stiff collar without a tie beneath their working apparel.

Next in line were the carpenters, who could be employed on building large construction and staging and any repair work. Along with shipwrights, they would make doors and frames and less intricate furniture ashore.

Plumbers mainly worked in lead and connected all the sanitary fittings that required lead piping to and from sinks and toilets. They would also deal with any gas piping that needed installing. Many pipes were joined by lead soldering.

The tinsmith worked in tin and spelter and the re-metalling of white metal bearing shells. Any tin and pewter utensils for manufacture and repair also fell to his trade. He was sometimes referred to as a 'tin basher'.

Coppersmiths could work in copper and brass, as all gauges were connected with copper tubing and all the pipes for flushing urinals were of copper. The onerous task of tubing condensers would come within their remit, alongside fitters. They could also be involved in the manufacture and repair of copper-riveted boilers and pressure vessels and fire extinguishers. The coppersmith was sometimes referred to as the 'pipe strangler'.

Pipefitters installed all the steel fresh water, salt water and steam piping, of which there were miles, ensuring any water/steam tightness between the flanges by fitting the right gaskets.

It will be seen that there were no welders during this era as this trade had not been fully tried, tested and developed. That said, in 1907 the workforce at the Harland & Wolff shipyard witnessed a display of the new technique of steel plate welding by the Thermite Company. Mention should also be made of the laggers and pipe laggers, two trades that evolved over this period. These craftsmen lagged the cylinder jackets and turbine casings to cut down on heat loss and improve thermal efficiency. This was done by mixing asbestos fibres with cement, which was then plastered on. Little did anyone realise at the time what a lethal legacy this left for the future health of shipyard workers.

On a more serious note, around the time of the Home Rule crisis there was an all-out targeted attack on Catholics or those with Nationalist or Republican sympathies. After 1920, Lord Pirrie and his Directors persuaded the workforce to accept Catholics provided they did not associate with Sinn Fein. This went ahead although the Joiners union did not accept it; however, they did with time and an unsettled peace prevailed in the Yard.

2. SCOTCH BOILERS – A WORKSHOP UNDER PRESSURE

A Boilermaker, the only trade to give its name to a drink – A pint of brown & mild

During the 1880s, vessels with a single boiler of pressure of 90 psi were being built, and by 1885 the engine works built its first triple expansion reciprocating engine for a vessel named the *Iran*, with a boiler pressure of 160 psi.

In 1895, Lord William Pirrie had succeeded Sir Edward Harland as Chairman of Harland & Wolff. As the sizes of ships increased, so their propulsive power also increased, the preferred style of boiler being the fire-tube cylindrical or Scotch boiler. By the end of the nineteenth century, the 17,000 gross ton *Oceanic*, the first ship which exceeded the length of the *Great Eastern*, entered service for the White Star Line. Her engines, which had a combined output of 28,000ihp, required fifteen double-ended Scotch boilers to provide steam at a pressure of 192 psi. The shell plates of the double-ended Scotch boilers were of special steel 1½in thick. Opposite furnaces were riveted to a common combustion chamber. It was a characteristic feature of Harland & Wolff steam machinery that the most ample boiler capacity was always provided, a feature to which the regular running of their vessels could be largely attributed.

When the *Olympic* trio were being built, each was installed with twenty-four double-ended and five single-ended Scotch boilers with a working pressure of 215 psi, somewhat of a high point for marine boilers at the time. All the boilers were hydraulically tested to twice their working pressure, i.e. 430 psi, to see if there were any leaks or seepage. They were of massive proportions, each double-ended boiler being 15ft 9in in diameter and 21ft in length. They could probably have fitted a char-à-banc of the day inside.

As previously discussed, the boilermakers riveted the boiler plates together. Whereas the ships' plate's holes had been punched out to accommodate the rivets, boiler plates being curved, were drilled radially in a pre-set-up drilling jig and the holes reamered out to remove any burrs or tears. This may be a good reason why boiler plates were not caulked.

A view through boilers. A four-furnace, double-ended Scotch boiler under construction in the Boiler Shop during November 1898. Through the right-hand furnace aperture is a boiler intended for White Star's *Oceanic* (II) of 1899. (Authors' collection)

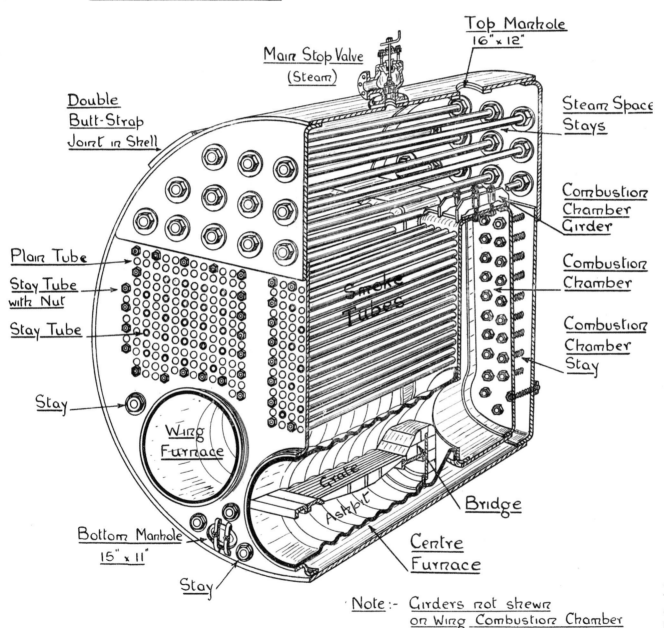

SINGLE-ENDED SCOTCH BOILER

Main Stop Valve (Steam)

Top Manhole 16" x 12"

Double Butt-Strap Joint in Shell

Steam Space Stays

Combustion Chamber Girder

Combustion Chamber

Combustion Chamber Stay

Plain Tube

Stay Tube with Nut

Stay Tube

Smoke Tubes

Stay

Wing Furnace

Grate

Ashpit

Bridge

Centre Furnace

Bottom Manhole 15" x 11"

Stay

Note:- Girders not shewn on Wing Combustion Chamber

A sketch showing the complex internal construction of a Scotch boiler. (Authors' collection)

Above: A four-furnace, single-ended boiler under construction at Swan Hunter on the Tyne, for Cunard's *Mauretania* of 1907. (Authors' collection)

Right: Boiler firebox and furnace. The boiler shop with furnaces and combustion chamber being built for the *Britannic* (II). It shows vertically positioned, two vertical furnaces with their bellows-like corrugation structures, to increase the heat exchanging area, fixed either side of their common combustion chamber, before being installed into the boiler shell. Lurking in the shadows may be seen a couple of boilermakers. (UF&TM)

The Boiler Shop in the Engineering Department c.1901, showing three-furnace, single-ended Scotch boilers destined for Holland America's *Noordam*. (John McMillan)

Left: Two rows of almost complete double-ended Scotch boilers for the *Olympic* in the boiler shop. These boilers, with their three-furnace fronts mounted, were built by the firm's workforce of boilermakers, now a very rare trade. The figure between the rows show how massive these structures were at 15ft 9in diameter and 21ft long. (UF&TM)

Opposite: Three-furnace, double-ended Scotch boilers destined for the *Britannic* (II) in the boiler shop. Below the nearest boiler is a stack of fire tubes and just by them some boiler stays which support the boiler internally. (David Hutchings collection)

Left: One of *Britannic* (II)'s 19½-ton boilers being hoisted ready for installation into the ship. (Authors' collection)

Below left: The Thor pneumatic caulker is here being used to caulk the seams of the riveted plate. This was a particularly noisy operation in an era when ear-defenders were unknown. (Authors' collection)

Below right: One of the twenty-four double-ended boilers being shipped aboard the *Britannic* (II) during March 1914. These huge vessels had to be installed on their mountings systematically to avoid the hull listing too much. Bad weather could delay this operation. (Harland & Wolff)

3. STEAM RECIPROCATING ENGINES AND TURBINES

In Engineering terms, a Camel is a Horse designed by committee.
The silhouette of a Camel was the original trademark of the Cammell Laird, Shipbuilders of Birkenhead.

Between White Star's second *Oceanic* of 1899 and the First World War, Harland & Wolff had built its greatest number of large ships, i.e. of gross tonnage 15,000 to 25,000, and over. Only twenty ocean-going merchant ships were below 450ft length, the greater number were 500ft to 650ft and above; several were over 700ft long. The largest quadruple-expansion engines were those for the *Adriatic* (II) of 1907. The opening years of the twentieth century saw the reciprocating steam engine reach the peak of its development; thereafter its eclipse was rapid, as the steam turbine gradually developed.

In Belfast, steam turbines became an integral part of a propulsion system peculiarly associated in the lay mind with Harland & Wolff. The *Laurentic* (I) (Yard No. 394) , 550ft long, completed in 1909, was the first of twenty-two triple-screw steamers to be built in which the wing (outer) shafts were driven by balanced four-crank triple-expansion engines and the centre shaft by a direct coupled low pressure turbine into which the reciprocators exhausted. For the same steam consumption, and on a lower machinery weight, triple-screw machinery showed 20 per cent power increase compared with twin-screw quadruple-expansion engines.

The *Olympic* and *Titanic* were the best examples of the triple-screw arrangement. Each wing engine developed 17,000ihp at 77 rev/min and the centre turbine 17,000shp at 165 rev/min. The third ship of this class, the *Britannic,* had a slightly larger turbine with blading length varying from 16in to 26½in. The casting, construction and blading of these turbines was of a specialist nature, with great precision needed in the fitting and balancing. The main engines were of such epic proportions, the height of a three-storey house of the day, and weighed 991 tons. They were the largest steam reciprocating engines ever built in the British Isles. With *Britannic,* triple-screw machinery reached its highest point.

The second *Laurentic* (II) (Yard No. 470), built in 1927, was the last of the type, and was an anachronism. It is rumoured that the International Mercantile Marine Co. which had originally ordered her did not want her by the time of her construction in the early 1920s.

By this time, due to the escalating cost of shipbuilding, the contract with Harland & Wolff was for the first time with White Star on a 'fixed price' basis and not on 'cost plus', as had been the previous arrangements. Apparently the *Laurentic*'s (by this time) rather outdated combination machinery had been stored for some five years prior to its installation. These may be some of the factors contributing to her delay.

The direct driven steam turbine was not a serious competitor with the reciprocator, other than for special services; it was a compromise between a fast moving turbine and a slow turning propeller. But the successful introduction of gearing by Parsons in 1910, whereby a high speed turbine was geared to a slow speed propeller, thus obtaining an efficient heat cycle and a high propulsive coefficient, completely changed the perspective. By the time the First World War started, the geared turbine was well established.

Returning to the *Laurentic* (II) of 1927, it is of interest to note an anecdote from a senior Cunard White Star engineer who joined her in 1939 before he was due to take his Second Class Certificate of Competency, who observed:

Above: The engine works Erection Shop during 1912. To the bottom right is an intermediate cylinder casting for the *Britannic* (II), with part of its engine bed on the left. (Authors' collection)

Opposite: The main Turning Shop in 1912, view looking east. Note the overhead main belt drive shaft supplying auxiliary shafts to the cone gearing that drive separate machines, mainly lathes. The lathe on the right would probably have had its own motor. (*Engineering*)

The engines were, of course, quite out of date by 1927 standards. Engaging the centre exhaust turbine and its propeller appeared to have little effect on the vessel's speed. One of the senior engineers, who knew the vessel, claimed it had no effect on the speed, but 'it took the knocks out of the engines'. Among the engineers were some ex-Cunarders who looked down their noses at the reciprocating engines, not to mention coal.

By then, the *Laurentic* was past its best.

In all, only twenty-two passenger ships were installed with Harland & Wolff's combination machinery.

The non-technically-minded reader should not feel intimidated by all the technical terms, but know that components were manufactured to such large dimensions and were part of the whole. Common terms like piston, piston rod, cylinder, cylinder cover, guide, crosshead, column, connecting rod, crank, crank-pin, crank-shaft, bearings and bedplate are all part of the technobabble of the lore of the steam engine.

The main Turning Shop in 1912 looking west. Heavy lifts were done by overhead cranes. The drive belts were made of either leather, webbing or balata and joined by an accessible buckle. At the height of the manufacturing day when a plethora of buckles clacked around the pulley wheels, the noise must have been loud and relentless. (*Engineering*)

The Smithy in the Engineering Department in 1912. The forges can be seen in the background with steam-operated hammers in the foreground. At the base of the near steam-operated hammer may be seen the foot-operated pedal which started the steam hammer to deliver its hammer blows. (*Engineering*)

The Brass Finishing Shop during 1912. In this shop brass sidelights/portholes and brass valves were cast, machined and assembled. Bronze propeller blades prior to building onto cast steel hubs would be fettled and buffed in this shop. (*Engineering*)

The *Olympic*'s LP turbine rotor in a lathe. The drum is ready to have grooves machined in it to locate the turbine blades. The *Olympic* and *Titanic*'s turbines were manufactured under licence at John Brown, Clydebank, and built by Harland & Wolff employees overseen by John Brown engineers. (David Hutchings collection)

Another view from a different angle of the blading of the *Olympic*'s turbine. (Authors' collection)

The *Olympic*'s turbine being fitted with rows of blades. This would be a prestigious job for top-class fitters as great precision and patience was required. (David Hutchings collection)

The *Olympic*'s turbine casing fitted together without the turbine rotor, possibly for boring out the bearing shell mountings and the labyrinth steam gland locations for the correct alignment. (Authors' collection)

The *Olympic*'s completed turbine assembly being installed
in the ship's turbine engine room during outfitting.
(UF&TM)

Left: The *Aquitania* at John Brown, Clydebank, supported on its keel blocks and shored up at the sides by massive wooden beams (shores). Here is a view under the almost finished hull. Note the chalk ticks by the rivets indicating that these are sound and watertight. At this stage she weighs 22,000 tons. (Authors' collection)

Below: Preparing to launch the *Aquitania*. Shipwrights are driving wedges beneath the ship to lift it from its keel blocks on which it has been built, to transfer its weight to the launching cradle, so that the ship may slip easily into the water. A highly labour-intensive task in which the shipwrights use their large 'mauls' to drive in the wedges. (Authors' collection)

Launch of the *Olympic* at Harland & Wolff on 20 October 1910. The hull was painted white so that the press photographers would capture the event at its best advantage, the *Olympic* being first of the class. (World Ship Society)

Following the launch, a small boat attends to attach the tow ropes to the tugs to dock the *Olympic* and to clear some of the cradle debris. (World Ship Society)

A rare view discovered from the Kempster Collection, taken from in front of the launching platform. *Titanic* is underway on 31 May 1911. Note the abundance of the gathered spectators in their Edwardian costume. (Steve Raffield)

The *Titanic* (right) and *Olympic* (left) together at Belfast for the last time on 6 March 1912. The *Olympic* returned for dry docking with the *Titanic* alongside at the Thompson deep water wharf. (Authors' collection)

The new Turbine Machinery and Erecting Shop in 1912. Note to the right the built-up propeller on its static balancing supports (knife edges). To its left is a small LP turbine casing and, to the left middle, what appears to be a bronze propeller blade. (*Engineering*)

The *Britannic* (II)'s completed turbine rotor suspended above the lower casing ready for installation. The vertical guide columns are erected in place to ensure the exact location of blading and bearings. The bowler-hatted foreman to the left oversees this delicate task. (UF&TM)

The turbine rotor of the *Britannic* (II) in the process of blading. This turbine was built in-house at Belfast and was a larger and improved modification of those built for the *Olympic* and *Titanic*. (Authors' collection)

The shaft of the *Olympic*'s rudder head being machined at The Darlington Forge Ltd in Darlington. Note the large counterbalance on the lathe's circular faceplate which clamps the shaft. Because of the length of the rudder head, to the right may be seen two 'steadies' to add extra bearing support. (Authors' collection)

The blading of a small turbine wheel in a blading jig at Swan Hunter's on the Tyne. (David Hutchings collection)

The Main Reciprocating Engine Erecting Shop in 1912. To the left is the bed and crankshaft for Bibby Line's *Oxfordshire* (Yard No. 429). On the right are engine support columns for White Star's *Ceramic* (Yard No. 432). (*Engineering*)

The *Ceramic* when completed in 1913 was the largest passenger ship on the Australian run and was dubbed 'The Queen of the Southern Ocean'. She was owned by White Star. Her sinking in the Second World War was with a heavy loss of life, with only a single survivor. (Authors' collection)

Above: The Machine Shop with huge planing and slotting machines in 1912. To the right is an engine bed casting for Royal Mail's *Andes* (I) (Yard No. 434) and a high-pressure cylinder casting for British & African S.N. Co.'s *Appam* (Yard No. 431). (*Engineering*)

Right: The *Titanic*'s starboard (left) and port (right) main engines. In the bottom right-hand corner may be seen the piston valves, 'D' slide valves and cylinder covers ready for assembly. (John McMillan)

End view of the *Titanic*'s port main engine under construction. It shows the LP cylinder and beneath it the toothed flywheel with the steam-driven turning gear engaged. In the foreground are two eccentric sheaves prior to fitting. (David Hutchings collection)

The Principal Moulding Bay in the Iron Foundry in 1912. Here the large sand moulds were made to take the patterns for the shape prior to casting. (*Engineering*)

The New Bay in the Iron Foundry in 1912. In this view there are two cupolas to the left and four cupolas in the distance. One of characteristics of the iron foundries was the all-pervading smell of sulphur from the casting process. Although foundry men could cope with the pungent odour, it also permeated their clothing. Travelling home from work on the trams it was safe to say that adjacent seating may have been vacant. (*Engineering*)

Opposite: Casting what may be a large propeller. This at best was a most dangerous job during the pouring of molten metal. The standing on the mould demonstrates a professional confidence. Sometimes gases could build up in the mould during pouring, causing a bursting out of the sand and molten metal. (Harland & Wolff)

Below: The turbine casing casting pit in the Foundry in 1912. The largest single components cast were the upper and lower casings of the low pressure exhaust turbines. This required a pit which was fed with successive molten metal. (*Engineering*)

The Brass Foundry in 1912. Here is where port brasses, small and large valve bodies, and any brass bearing shells would be cast. It is also the shop where the bronze propeller blades were cast. The team to the left are about to remove a freshly cast blade from its mould box, while there is a man on the extreme right 'fettling' a blade to improve its surface finish. All are watched over by a bowler-hatted foreman. (*Engineering*)

A Single Reduction geared turbine set, for moderate steam pressures, with gear cases removed. At the top left is the high-pressure turbine; on the right is the low-pressure turbine. In the foreground is the thrust block. Without any person in the picture it is hard to get any idea of scale but these sets were larger than they look. (Harland & Wolff)

4. AT NEARBY WORKMAN, CLARK'S YARD

Known locally as the 'wee yard'.

Workman, Clark & Company was formed in 1880 by two former Harland & Wolff Premium Apprentices, Francis Workman and George Clark. They set up their shipbuilding yard directly opposite that of Harland & Wolff, and were therefore well known to Harland & Wolff's regular customers. They were in an ideal position to capture some of the business for themselves. The firm progressed and expanded slowly, with reputable shipping companies like T. & J. Harrison, Alfred Holt & Co., Cunard, China Mutual Steam Navigation Co. Ltd and Lamport & Holt placing orders with them. By 1901, for the first time, the 'wee yard' had produced more tonnage than their rival.

With a plethora of orders the yard prospered, and by the end of 1902 the tonnage returns showed the company to be at the head of the list of the world's shipbuilders, with a total gross tonnage of 86,712, including those under construction. The total displacement of vessels built by Workman, Clark amounted to nigh on 2 million tons.

Returning to the matter of the steam turbine as a prime mover, in the early part of the twentieth century the technology was not so advanced as that of steam reciprocating machinery. The turbine was better balanced and offered reduced risk of vibration; in addition, a turbine installation could occupy less space.

The major North Atlantic shipping company Allan Line took a leap of faith when it ordered the *Victorian* (Yard No. 206) from Workman, Clark, which was the firm's first passenger liner, and the first ocean-going-turbine driven liner. Not only did Workman, Clark build the 10,635 gross ton ship, but it also built the Parsons' steam turbines under licence. It is recorded that George Clark took a personal interest in its construction and she was launched on 25 August 1904.

The *Victorian*'s total engine output of some 12,000shp was developed by three turbines being directly connected to the three screw shafts. In order to obtain a reasonable propulsive efficiency at the ship's designed speed of 17.5 knots, the propeller speed, and that of the turbine, had to be 290 rev/min maximum. Steam velocity through a nozzle was high and so turbine speed had to be high. In order to allow for a relatively low rotational speed, it was necessary to fit turbines of large diameters, and that system remained with all directly connected turbines.

The HP turbine weighed 60 tons, while the two LP turbines each weighed 100 tons, steam was supplied to them at 185 psi by eight Scotch boilers.

The *Victorian* entered service on 10 March 1905, and that year the shipyard delivered the *Matatua* (Yard No. 205), a refrigerated cargo ship for Shaw Savill & Albion's New Zealand meat trade, and also laid down the banana boats *Pacuare* and *Zent* (Yard Nos 221 & 222) for Elders & Fyffes.

Between 1905 and 1913, Workman, Clark launched a hundred vessels whose tonnage was 83 per cent of the seventy-five ships built by Harland & Wolff in Belfast. They also beat their neighbour's output in 1907, 1910 and 1913.

In 1918, Mr John Moir, one of the company's riveters, set a personal record by driving home a total of 11,209 rivets over a nine-hour shift!

Workman, Clark ceased trading in 1935. Subsequently its South Yard and the engine works were taken over by Harland & Wolff, and the rest of the establishment dismantled. Many of its workforce were absorbed into Harland & Wolff.

The *City of Agra* (Yard No. 203), a 4,808-gross-ton cargo ship completed for Ellerman Line Ltd Steamship Co. in 1903. She was driven by steam reciprocating machinery. (Authors' collection)

The power station in the Engineering Department. This power supply would be independent of Belfast city's 'Electric Light Works' in order to power all the lighting in the various workshops and to power the giant motor that drove the overhead belt drive shaft continuously and uninterruptedly. This would require its own service personnel to run and maintain it known as the 'works engineers'. (*Engineering*)

This photo shows the massive planing machine made by Hunton & Co. of Manchester. Its main function was to machine a component clamped to a movable bed (the platen) relative to the stationary tool to remove metal. In this view it appears that the support column of a reciprocating engine is mounted on its side having its foot machined. (*Engineering*)

The crankshaft lathe in the Engineering Department, made by Thomas Shanks & Co. of Johnstone. The turning of the crankshaft bearing journals was a delicate task undertaken by a top-class craftsman, as shown standing adjacent to the large circular chuck. There is a large counterweight clamped on the chuck to counterbalance the crank-web. Note the drive belt to the rear of the chuck and the respective gearing. This is a posed photograph as the man would not be standing in this position with the lathe and crankshaft being turned. (*Engineering*)

Above: The crank-web boring machine (left) and slotting machine (centre) in the Engineering Department. The boring machine seems idle in this image but there is a bearing shell or similar component in the slotting machine ready for finished machining. These were used to finish machine the large webs which were shrunk onto the crank in order to build up the crankshaft. The ladder gives an idea of scale. Note in an era before health and safety the lack of any guards or rails around these machines. (*Engineering*)

Left: General view of the Finishing Shop in the Engineering Department. The building was constructed of corrugated iron with a total height of 75ft. On either side of this photo may be seen the fitters' workstations complete with heavy-duty vices. It was a cathedral-like building with high windows to let in the natural light. On the centre of the shop floor are piston connecting rods and an array of bearing shells awaiting assembly. (*Engineering*)

Left: Blading turbines in the Engineering Department. This view is of the Allan liner *Victorian*'s partly bladed low-pressure rotor and casing (Yard No. 206). Blading was a real precision task requiring skill and patience from the top tradesmen. (*Engineering*)

Below: Turning Shop in the Engineering Department. Served by overhead cranes, to the upper left may be seen the main overhead belt drive shaft serving the individual auxiliary shafts to the lathes, this is not so obvious on the right-hand side. In the lathe to the far right is a crankshaft clamped to a chuck for bearing machining. On the shop floor are various solid and hollow shafts in differing stages of finish. Near the foreground is a shiny multi-collared shaft for a thrust block. (*Engineering*)

A general view in the Boiler Shop with the jigs holding a single-ended boiler to the left. The jigs are holding the boilers so that the four-headed radial drilling machine may drill the holes in adjacent plates to be joined by rivets. This was another process requiring precision and accuracy. The boilermaker standing next to the machine gives some scale to the size of these vessels. (*Engineering*)

A contemporaneous image of two riveters at work in an unidentified yard. Note their rig of waistcoat with voluminous shirtsleeves to give them the maximum of unrestricted movement. Their hammers would be superseded by the pneumatic and hydraulic riveting machines. This would have spared their aching muscles. (David Hutchings collection)

5. PRE-WAR TIMES AT HARLAND & WOLFF

The Foremen and Managers wore bowler hats because they were atop their trade,
While Orangemen wear them annually when marching on parade.

In 1906, Gustav Wolff retired from the shipyard and William Pirrie became controlling chairman, and in that year he was created Baron Pirrie.

In order to accommodate such large ships of the 'Olympic' class, Sir William Arrol of the Glasgow steel construction firm was contracted to build the Arrol Gantry which straddled Nos 2 and 3 slipways, at a cost of £100,000. Four electric lifts and many ramps gave the workforce access to the whole structure. This was completed in early 1908 and later, on 16 December that year, the keel of the *Olympic* was laid. With these in place, the firm had a total of eight building slips.

As well as the Arrol Gantry, another massive structure was contracted for. In 1904, construction of the Thompson Graving (Dry) Dock was commenced, eventually completed in 1911 at a cost of £350,000.

The output from British shipyards showed a dramatic decline in 1908. The unprecedented production of 1906 gave way to a drop of just over 10 per cent in 1907, to a total of 1.6 million gross registered tons. But in 1908 that figure was almost halved to 930,000 tons, and the following year it rose slightly to 991,000 tons. In 1910 the total rose, but it was not until 1911 that the full effects of the depression in the industry were over.

Between 1908 and 1912 work on the *Olympic* and *Titanic* progressed, but at the same time there were other ships under construction in the Yard. For White Star there was the *Zealandic* (Yard No. 421), *Nomadic* (Yard No. 422) and *Traffic* (Yard No. 423); for Royal Mail the *Deseado* (Yard No. 420); the *Appam* (Yard No. 431) for British & African SS Co.; and the *Katoomba* (Yard No. 437) for McIlwraith, McEachan of Adelaide.

In 1910, the following ships were launched:

Edinburgh Castle	13,326grt	Union-Castle (Yard No. 410)
Pakeha	7,911	Shaw Savill (Yard No. 409)
Gloucestershire	8,124	Bibby Line (Yard No. 411)
Themistocles	11,500	Aberdeen Line (Yard No. 412)
Olympic	45,500	White Star (Yard No. 400)
Sachsen	8,250	Hamburg Amerika Line (Yard No. 413)
Bayern	8,250	Hamburg Amerika Line (Yard No. 416)
Maloja	13,000	P&O (Yard No. 414)

In all a total of 115,861grt. There was a total workforce of 13–14,000 employed at Harland & Wolff, while at nearby Workman, Clark the workforce was 9,000.

Against this backdrop of these seeming boom years, Harland & Wolff was badly affected by the *Titanic* disaster of April 1912, and the death of Thomas Andrews. In 1913 Gustav Wolff died, and so did John Pierpont Morgan, the head of the International Mercantile Marine Company, holding group of the White Star Line.

Harland & Wolff's Chief Naval Architect, Alexander Carlisle, who was responsible for the design of the 'Olympic' class, quit in the middle of the fitting out of the *Olympic* and the construction of the *Titanic*; he was later appointed as the Company's Managing Director on 1 January 1914.

The third of the 'Olympic'-class trio, the *Britannic* (II), was launched on 26 February 1914 and was lauded as 'The largest British built vessel'. On 21 November 1916, she struck a mine in the Kia Channel in the Aegean Sea and sunk with the loss of twenty-eight lives. She was the largest British merchant ship to be sunk in the two world wars.

Union-Castle's *Edinburgh Castle* (II) (Yard No. 410) positioned alongside the jetty after her launch on 27 January 1910. (Alan Mallett collection)

As Belfast entered the First World War and much construction was diverted to warship building, Harland & Wolff's yard covered 135 acres and its workforce expanded to 18,000, while Workman, Clark's increased to 12,000.

During the First World War, Lord Pirrie was appointed Controller-General of Merchant Shipbuilding. Pirrie was responsible for the laying down at Belfast of an entirely new and extensive shipyard with six large slips for building standard merchant ships. The yard, which became the Musgrave Yard or the East Yard, increased the potential output of the firm to a considerable extent, and was the birthplace of large ships for many of the premier shipping companies of the day. Also during this time he championed the removal of trade demarcation boundaries where it was possible.

Another feature that became the hallmark of Harland & Wolff's design was the change in the ships' stern from the traditional counter stern to the 'cruiser' stern. The original intention of the cruiser stern was to enable the steering gear to be housed below the protective decks in warships. It quickly became apparent that this idea considerably lengthened the waterline, and thus improved the efficiency of the propulsion. Further, part of the stern became waterborne, thus increasing the ship's displacement, and hence its deadweight, without any alterations in overall dimensions. Moreover, a partially buoyant stern meant that the ship would ride more easily to a following sea. These advantages, coupled with a slight gain in carrying space, made the idea very attractive to Harland & Wolff's designers, and following the First World War more and more passenger ships adopted this form of stern.

Above right: The *Olympic* in the Thompson dry dock showing the damage to the starboard propeller and hull plate damage caused during her collision with HMS *Hawke* in September 1911. (UF&TM)

Below right: Work in progress on fitting an extended watertight inner shell in the *Olympic* in December 1912. These were recommended modifications to enhance her watertight integrity following the *Titanic* disaster. (Authors' collection)

The *Britannic* (II)'s starboard intermediate propeller shaft mounted in the lathe in the process of being machined. At either end of the shaft are the forged flanges that will need to be drilled for the coupling bolts. This photo was taken with the lathe stopped and the shaft stationary. The two turners to the extreme left are checking that the process will be machined accurately. (Authors' collection)

Left: The *Britannic* (II)'s port main engine finished in the works. Under the large steam 'eduction' pipe to the left is the shiny vertical connecting link to the reversing 'weighshaft' of which one of its links is near to the camera. (Authors' collection)

Below: Another view of *Britannic* (II)'s port main engine while under construction. At the base of the engine are the half shells of the white metal journal bearings. (Authors' collection)

The *Britannic* (II)'s complete port main engine along with its starboard one, each weighing 1,000 tons. The engineer on the engine top gives some idea of the massive size of these propulsion units. To the right are the engines being built for Holland America's *Statendam* (I) (Yard No. 436), later *Justicia*, in an early stage of construction. (NMNI)

The *Britannic* (II) under construction. In the picture may be seen a craftsman, probably a burner, using an oxy-acetylene flame cutting torch. Welding at this time had not been introduced into shipyards. The large apertures are the localities of the boiler uptakes where the flue gases will leave to the funnels. These holes in the deck were working hazards not roped off. (Authors' collection)

Above: The *Britannic* (II) on the stocks prior to her launch on 26 February 1914. At this time the Harland & Wolff yard was plagued by a flock of starlings which roosted in the gantries at night. The mess from their droppings was not only unsightly but so slippery as to be actually dangerous to the squad of men working. Therefore, a gang of workmen were brought in early at about 5.30 each morning to wash it away with high-pressure hoses before the main labour force arrived. Note the stock steel plate in the foreground ready for plating future builds or in case steel supply was interrupted during the war years. (Harland & Wolff-Robert Welch)

Above: A wide image of the *Britannic* (II) under construction with an unobstructed view of the hydraulic riveting machine being operated by two riveters. Note the cohorts of rivets completed in joining the plates to the frames. The two chalk marks could be quality inspection marks. (Authors' collection)

Right: The *Titanic*'s starboard tailshaft being installed from outside the ship before her launch. Note that the rudder has been secured by braces in order to keep it in the midships position during the launch. Behind the shaft may be seen the bowler hat of the foreman overseeing this delicate task. Also, the 'ghost' of a workman who has been 'airbrushed' from the negative. There seems to be no safety net or line for the worker adjusting the nut on the end of the tailshaft. (Authors' collection)

Two liners that were war losses, preventing them from entering commercial service. Here they are photographed 'born' together, the *Britannic* (II) is on slipway No. 2 on the right and to the left is the *Statendam* (I) (Yard No. 436) on slipway No. 3. (NMNI)

The tank top and double bottom of Red Star Line's *Nederland* (Yard No. 469), seen from its bow on Harland & Wolff's No. 2 slipway on 20 May 1914. Work was started on this passenger ship as soon as the *Britannic* had vacated the slipway. (Harland & Wolff-Robert Welch)

Left: Riveters at work on the *Nederland* using the pneumatic riveting machine. This photo shows what confined conditions they are working in. The riveter below is the holder-up and he is using the pneumatic 'dolly' to resist the force from the riveting machine above. (NMNI)

Opposite: Stern view of Red Star Line's *Belgenland* (Yard No. 391), on No. 1 slipway at Harland & Wolff prior to her hurried launch on 31 December 1914. This was so the vacated slipway could be used for prioritised naval construction. The hawse pipe for a stern anchor is a dominant feature. Note the rudder has not been fitted. (Harland & Wolff-Robert Welch)

The keel structure of the *Homeric* (ex-*Germanic*, Yard No. 470) on slipway No. 3, probably showing the greatest extent of her construction. This was before her second removal incomplete in December 1917. (Harland & Wolff-Robert Welch)

Another view of Harland & Wolff's slipway No. 3 and the keel of the *Homeric* (Yard No. 470), seen either while under construction or demolition. (Harland & Wolff-Robert Welch)

Boring out the cylinder for the piston of the *Britannic* (II)'s port changeover valve. This large boring machine was made in Scotland by Thomas Shanks & Co. of Johnstone. The rotating cutter was driven by the huge horizontal geared wheel at the top. The machinist could alter the depth of cut manually on the tool head by adjusting it before the tool was fed into the bore. Note on the bedplate are a set of internal callipers to check the dimension of the bore. (Authors' collection)

The casing of one of *Olympic*'s changeover valves in the engine works. (UF&TM)

The installation of the main engines into the *Britannic* (II). After test running them in the main engine shop, the engines were disassembled and rebuilt up from the bedplate in the ship. An end of a crankshaft is in place on the engine room bedplates. Main bearings are in place and the open flat plates show where the main engine support columns were to be located. On the stairs is the dark bowler-hatted figure of a foreman overseeing the outfitting. (Authors' collection)

The motor vessel *Lautaro* (ex-*Bostonian*), built as the *Glengyle* by Harland & Wolff, Govan, and precursor to the extensive construction of diesel-powered ships that followed at Belfast. (Clyde Ships)

The *Britannic* (II) at Belfast before being taken up for trade, berthed with the naval monitors that were built in place of the *Germanic* and *Nederland*. The four funnels of the *Olympic* can be seen in the background of this photo dating from around July 1915. At that time, the *Britannic*'s lifeboats had not been shipped and she appears to be painted in White Star's livery. (Bruce Beveridge)

6. BUSY YARD BUT LEAN TIMES AHEAD

When the last ship goes, the great yard will close.

In 1912, Harland & Wolff's interest in diesel engines took a more practical form when the Danish firm Burmeister & Wain Oil Engine Company became established at Finnieston, Glasgow, on a site that Harland & Wolff had already acquired. One third of the new company's capital was held by Harland & Wolff and the remainder by Burmeister & Wain of Copenhagen.

At the outbreak of war in 1914, Harland & Wolff became the sole proprietor of the Finnieston Company, and from these early beginnings great advances were soon made in the application of the diesel engine to marine propulsion. The first two motor ships to be built by Harland & Wolff were the *Glenartney* and *Glengyle* (Yard Nos 467 & 466) for Glen Line in 1915.

White Star's *Vedic* (Yard No. 461), which entered service in 1918, was the first Harland & Wolff-built ship to be fitted with single reduction geared turbines that developed 3,600shp.

At the end of the First World War, the British shipyards were working to full capacity to replace vessels that were lost during the war. During 1918, Harland & Wolff completed 201,070 gross tons of merchant vessels, 120,000 tons more than their nearest rivals. Over 120 were built between 1918 and 1924, a very comfortable position for the yard to be in. Northern Ireland was very prosperous in the twenties, but unfortunately it was not shared with all the inhabitants. This immediate post-war period encouraged the enlargement and improvement of the company's shipbuilding capabilities. These remained incomplete when Lord Pirrie died in 1924, by which time orders had greatly diminished.

Lord Kylsant, Chairman of the Royal Mail Group, which included such shipping lines as Royal Mail Line, Shaw Savill, Union-Castle and later White Star, became Chairman of Harland & Wolff in 1924, a position he held for six years. In this time, Harland & Wolff was reconstituted as a public company and further orders were received from the Royal Mail Group, financed by loans granted under the Trades Facilities Acts, as was part of the Yard's modernisation. The construction of main diesel engines was also commenced at Queen's Island from 1925 onwards.

Notable among passenger ships to have diesel engines installed in the latter half of that decade were the large double-acting, four-stroke engines for the twin-screw Royal Mail ships *Asturias* (II) and *Alcantara* (II) (Yard Nos 507 & 586) of 15,000bhp. Then came the first of a Union-Castle series designed for the 'express' service to the Cape, the *Carnarvon Castle* (Yard No. 595), a vessel of 20,000grt and 13,000bhp.

The series of large passenger ships with the double-acting, four-stroke machinery reached its peak as the 1930s approached, with the 27,000grt *Britannic* (III) and *Georgic* (II) (Yard Nos 807 & 896); these latter two were the last liners built for the White Star Line.

Lord Kylsant was forced to resign from the chairman's post due to financial irregularities that affected both companies. Sir Frederick Rebbeck was appointed chairman in 1930 and held the position for over thirty years, until he had to retire due to ill health. The first ship notably to be launched under his tenure in 1931 was the *Georgic* (qv) of 27,267 gross tons, for White Star. But he also had to deal with all the problems that were created by his predecessor. The Wall Street Crash of 1929 that rocked the industrialised world was to follow. The yard was badly affected, orders were cancelled, the yard stood idle, there was a threat of closure. In 1932, ironically when the *Georgic* was completed, thousands of Belfast workers were unemployed, only surviving on Outdoor Relief, a meagre 16s (80p) a week for a family of four.

At this crisis in their affairs the Northern Ireland government came to Harland & Wolff's rescue, and offered very easy terms of finance (the Trades Facilities Acts) for any shipowners who placed orders with the company. The management at Shaw Savill & Albion seized this opportunity. They ordered not one but three refrigerated cargo vessels. The three sisters, the *Waiwera*, *Waipawa* and *Wairangi* (Yard Nos 922, 923 & 924) were at the time the largest and fastest cargo ships that were built for Shaw Savill at a cost of just over £1 million. Each was installed with twin diesel engines of 11,000bhp, had an overall length of 535ft, with a refrigerated cargo capacity of over half a million tons and a service speed of 16½ knots. From 1934 up until the Second World War, they proved to be the biggest money earners Shaw Savill ever had built for them.

It is of interest to note that between 1915 and 1932 some 111 motorships were built for the Royal Mail Group. Harland & Wolff were in crisis, but they had survived changes of management, the First World War and the partition of Ireland in 1921 whereby the Irish Free State was formed. Fortunately, at this time when six counties became Northern Ireland, Belfast was a major commercial and industrial centre and was not greatly impacted by the change.

Union-Castle's *Arundel Castle* (III) following her launch on 11 September 1919. Her hull was laid down on No. 3 slipway on 11 November 1915 (Yard No. 455), but with wartime construction taking precedence and indecision regarding whether to complete her as a troop transport or auxiliary cruiser, her launch was delayed. She was installed with geared turbines and was the first ship to be so in the fleet, and entered service in 1921. She was also built with a cruiser stern. (Alan Mallett collection)

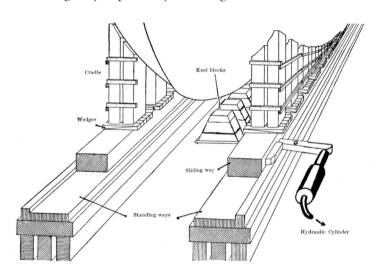

This drawing gives an idea of the method of launching. In the centre are the keel blocks. All stress has been taken off them when the whole weight was transferred to the slipways on either side. This was done by knocking the wedges in under the cradle. The cradle supporting the ship is now ready to slip down. Only the trigger prevents it from moving. When the trigger is released, the ship will slide down the slipway by itself. (Authors' collection)

The *Arundel Castle* was completed with four funnels, the last four-funnelled ship built by Harland & Wolff. This view shows the nest of lifeboats stowed in her gantry davits abaft the fourth funnel. She was modernised in 1937 and sold for demolition in 1958. (Alan Mallett collection)

Above: The yard in 1925, a pilot vessel is berthed in the Hamilton dry dock. (Authors' collection)

Left: White Star's only geared turbine-driven ship, the *Vedic*, a wartime emergency standard ship moored alongside at Harland & Wolff in 1925. Constructed at the company's Govan Yard, (No. 461) with engineering outfit work completed at Belfast, she was originally built essentially as a cargo ship and launched on 18 December 1917. (Authors' collection)

Left: Another image of the *Vedic* at the Harland & Wolff shipyard in 1925. She was at Belfast for a refit to suit her for the Australian emigrant service via South Africa. Following White Star's merger with Cunard in 1934, she was sold in July that year for demolition at Rosyth. (Authors' collection)

Below: The *Barrels* light vessel alongside at Harland & Wolff during 1924, one of many smaller ships that were maintained and refitted by the firm. (Authors' collection)

A typical shipyard scene in 1924, multiple cranes viewed from one of the yard's basins. (Authors' collection)

The Abercorn Basin at Harland & Wolff's shipyard in 1924. This basin, along with the adjacent Hamilton dry dock, was officially opened on 2 October 1867 when James Hamilton, Marquis of Abercorn, Lord Lieutenant-General and Governor General of Ireland named these facilities. Today the Hamilton dry dock is occupied by the fully restored passenger tender *Nomadic*, completed in 1911. (Authors' collection)

The North Yard gantry at Harland & Wolff during 1925. (Authors' collection)

Holland America's second *Statendam* (II) alongside at Harland & Wolff in 1924. This liner was ordered as a replacement to the first ship of the same name, completed in 1917 and sunk as the *Justicia*. She was ordered as Yard No. 612 in 1921 and launched from No. 14 slipway in the East Yard on 11 September 1924, about the same time that the United States introduced laws restricting immigration into the US. This caused work on the ship to be suspended. In addition to this, because of a series of strikes in the shipyard, the vessel was towed over to the Wilton-Fijenoord shipyard in Schiedam, where she was completed in March 1929. (Authors' collection)

The Great Gantry in Harland & Wolff's shipyard, originally built to construct the 'Olympic'-class trio. Originally known as the Arrol Gantry, in later years it cost the firm £40,000 a year to maintain and was demolished in the mid-1960s. (Authors' collection)

The rather dilapidated company sign marking the sea-wise entrance to Harland & Wolff's shipyard. Due to neglect and with priority given to wartime construction, by 1925 it was in much need of refurbishment. (Authors' collection)

Above: The giant floating crane built by the German firm of Deschimag A.G. and the Arrol Gantry in 1925 as seen from the River Lagan. (Authors' collection)

Right: A Royal Mail vessel's keel being laid in 1923. Although this is the only information on this image, it could be Royal Mail Line's *Lochmonar* (Yard No. 517) on Slipway No. 9 in the East Yard. A cargo ship of 9,463grt and one of the first Royal Mail ships be powered by diesel engines, she was broken up in 1949. (Authors' collection)

Opposite left: Men riveting frames at Harland & Wolff's East Yard. (Authors' collection)

Opposite right: Riveting the bottom of a ship. (Authors' collection)

An unnamed ship on the stocks. (Authors' collection)

Shipyard workshops and sheds looking down the road at the Arrol Gantry in the distance. (Authors' collection)

The launch of Union-Castle's *Carnarvon Castle* (III) (Yard No. 595) from No. 11 slipway in the East Yard on 14 January 1926. (Alan Mallett collection)

The *Carnarvon Castle* (III) after her launch, being taken in tow. She was the first of a series of large liners on the South African service, and after the steam-driven *Arundel* and *Windsor Castles* built for the company, was the first of Union-Castle's motor ships. She returned to the builders for reconstruction in November 1937. She survived the Second World War as an Armed Merchant Cruiser and later as a troopship and was scrapped in 1962. (Alan Mallett collection)

A view of the back of one of the *Carnarvon Castle*'s main engines. They were Harland & Wolff-built Burmeister & Wain 8-cylinder, 4-stroke, double-acting diesel engines. Each had a bore of 33in and a stroke of 59in and delivered 6,500bhp. Royal Mail's *Asturias* and *Alcantara* were fitted with the same engines. For their massive size, these engines were later in the 1960s referred to as 'Cathedral Diesels' or 'stone crushers'. (Alan Mallett collection)

Above: Starboard bow view of the *Accra* (Yard No. 616) on No. 9 slipway in the East Yard, prior to her launch on 17 August 1926. Although a significant occasion for both builders and ship owners, the following series has a rather eerie look with a seemingly deserted yard. (Authors' collection)

Right: A stern view of the *Accra* before her launch. She had been ordered for the British & African Steam Navigation Co. Ltd (Elder Dempster & Co. Ltd). (Authors' collection)

Left: The stern of the *Accra* enters the water following her launch on 17 August 1925. (Authors' collection)

Below: The *Accra*'s port quarter photographed passing during the launch. Her service with Elder Dempster took her on regular liner voyages between Liverpool and West Africa. (Authors' collection)

Left: The *Accra*'s full port view as she enters the water. She was engined with twin Harland & Wolff-built Burmeister & Wain 8-cylinder, 4-stroke, double-acting diesel engines. Each engine had bores of 26¾in and stroke of 55⅛in and developed 3,250bhp. (Authors' collection)

Below: A three-quarter-bow view of the *Accra* following her launch. The tug is positioned in the foreground after the *Accra*'s launch, as the ship's momentum comes to rest. (Authors' collection)

Left: The bow view of the *Accra* after her launch. She was later torpedoed on 26 July 1940 by a German submarine near Rockall with a loss of nineteen lives. (Authors' collection)

Below: The empty No. 9 slipway in the East Yard. (Authors' collection)

Top left: A mast being built in the workshop for White Star's *Laurentic* (II) (Yard No. 470), then under construction on slipway No. 3, during 1925. Due to its cylindrical construction, the work of riveting was carried out by boilermakers. (Authors' collection)

Centre left: Royal Mail's *Alcantara* (II) (Yard No. 586), a starboard view on No. 12 slipway in the East Yard prior to her launch on 23 September 1926. (Authors' collection)

Bottom left: Royal Mail's *Alcantara* in position, showing the fore poppet of her cradle in readiness for launching. (Authors' collection)

Below: The photographer has moved around and snapped the after cradle of the *Alcantara* just prior to her launch. (Authors' collection)

Above: A view of the *Alcantara*'s port stern quarter ready for launching. During outfitting she would be engined with the same prime movers as the *Carnarvon Castle*, developing the same power. (Authors' collection)

Right: A bow view of the *Alcantara* on Slipway No. 12 in readiness for her launching. (Authors' collection)

Left: A view of the *Alcantara*'s cruiser stern and propellers prior to her launching. (Authors' collection)

Below: The *Alcantara* during launching on 23 September 1926, here showing the stern entering the water, the transition from the slip to the sea, her working environment, for the first time. (Authors' collection)

Above left: Another photograph taken during the *Alcantara*'s launching. (Authors' collection)

Above right: The wash created by the *Alcantara*'s displacement as she is waterborne. (Authors' collection)

Left: The tugs are positioned ready to arrest the momentum of the *Alcantara* after launching. (Authors' collection)

A full bow view of the *Alcantara* following her launch. She survived the Second World War and was eventually sold for scrap in May 1958 for £240,000. She was the first large vessel sold for breaking up in Japan after the war. (Authors' collection)

Another view of her with tugs. Although fitted with the same diesel engines as the *Carnarvon Castle* and the *Asturias*, the *Alcantara* would return to Harland & Wolff in November 1934 to be re-engined with single reduction geared turbines of 20,000shp. (Authors' collection)

Above: Vacant Slipway No. 12 and cranes in the East Yard after the *Alcantara*'s launch. (Authors' collection)

Right: One of Royal Mail's *Asturias*'s (II) (Yard No. 507) main engines in the engine shop prior to installation into the ship during 1926. (Authors' collection)

Another view of one of the *Asturias*'s main engines. The Harland & Wolff-built, Burmeister & Wain, 8-cylinder, 4-stroke, double-acting diesel engine was very large and a complex piece of machinery. Sea-going experience on these engines was quite rare! (Authors' collection)

One of the main engine silencers destined for one of the *Asturias*'s main engines. Their combined output of 14,000bhp could sustain a service speed of 16 knots. (Authors' collection)

The second *Laurentic* (II) (Yard No. 470) of 1927. She was reputed to be the last coal-burning liner on the North Atlantic and the last passenger ship to be installed with Harland & Wolff's triple-screw combination machinery. (Tom Rayner collection)

A half-length of one of the massive balanced crankshafts of the motor vessel *Britannic* (III) in 1929, mounted in the lathe in the Main Engine Assembly Shop. It appears to be stationary, possibly ready for finish machining of the main bearing journals which had to be done at low rotational speeds. This task required great precision and competence on behalf of the operator or turner. After thirty years' service, severe fatigue cracks appeared in one of the *Britannic*'s crankshafts. (Harland & Wolff)

Launch of *Britannic* (III) (Yard No. 807) on 6 August 1929 from No. 1 slipway. (UF&TM)

The *Britannic* (III)'s main port engine completed in the builder's Engine Shop. It is linked up to a dynamometer to measure its brake horsepower. The engines were each 10-cylinder, 4-stroke, double-acting diesels with a combined output of 17,000bhp. (UF&TM)

The Launch of the *Britannic* (III). (Authors' collection)

The *Britannic* (III) docked in the Thompson Graving Dock at Belfast. She continued in service with Cunard White Star (later Cunard Steamship Company) after 1934 and served that company until sold for scrap in 1960. (Authors' collection)

Launch of Nelson Lines' *Highland Princess* (Yard No. 814) on 11 April 1929 from slipway No. 10 in the East Yard. She was later absorbed into the Royal Mail Lines and was sold to the Peoples' Republic of China in 1960. She was scrapped early in the 1980s. (Authors' collection)

Launch of the Elders & Fyffes 5,833grt banana boat *Musa* on 29 March 1930 from Workman, Clark's yard (Yard No. 515). This image is from a contemporary newspaper report of the day. Her propulsion was unique in that it was turbo-electric, thus dispensing with cumbersome gearing and turbine astern blading. She was completed as the *Contessa*. (Authors' collection)

Princess Mary, Countess Lascelles, visiting the keel structure of the *Oceanic* (III) (Yard No. 844) on slipway No. 14 in the East Yard on 15 October 1928. This liner, the third of the name for White Star, would have been the first vessel of 1,000ft with a gross tonnage of 60,000. (Pathé News)

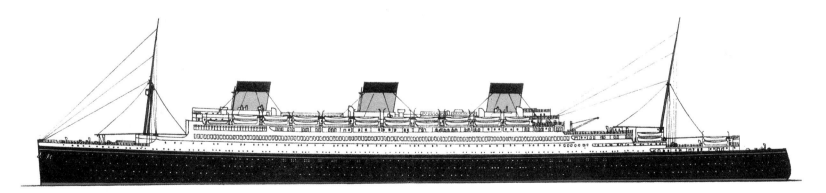

Captain John H. Isherwood's profile of how he perceived the *Oceanic* (III) would eventually appear. Due to the slow progress and impending Depression, the project was cancelled. (Authors' collection)

Union-Castle's *Warwick Castle* (II) (Yard No. 840) on slipway No. 12 in the East Yard just prior to her launch on 29 April 1930. On 12 November 1942 she was torpedoed by a German U-boat while nearing Gibraltar. (Alan Mallett collection)

The *Georgic* (II) (Yard No. 896), White Star's last liner, under construction on slipway No. 1 in early November 1930. She was launched a year later on 12 November 1931. Note the frame and beam construction, the hydraulic riveting calliper hanging in the distance. Two gangs of pneumatic riveters are nearest to camera with the rivet furnace between them. The man to the right is communicating to the holder-up beneath the deck. Note his right knee is cushioned for this repetitive work. But what is the workman on the extreme left doing? (Authors' collection)

The *Georgic* (II). When she entered service, for a while she was the largest motorship in the world at 27,759grt. In July 1941 she was bombed and sunk at Port Tewfik. She was salvaged and used mainly on trooping voyages until she was sold for scrap in January 1956. (B. & A. Feilden)

The *Waipawa* (Yard No. 923), Shaw Savill's large refrigerated cargo vessel on slipway No. 2, ready for her launch on 28 June 1934. (Authors' collection)

The completed *Waipawa*. One of a class of five that survived the war, after thirty-three years' service she was sold by the company in 1967 to the Greeks and re-named *Aramis*. She was scrapped in Taiwan in 1969. (B. & A. Feilden)

7. SHIPYARD 'BOGS'

'If you're not completely confused then you don't fully understand the situation.'
(Graffiti seen on a Public Convenience wall during 'The Troubles')

Throughout Britain, shipyard toilets were much the same style in every yard: stalls lined up battery-hen style, some with western saloon-style doors such that one's legs could be seen below the doors, and a large gap at the top that some unexpected foreman could peer over to see if a person was skiving. The lines of toilets were holes in boards over a long continuous, galvanised steel trough through which a common flush operated to take away the soil. The flushed soil probably ended up in the River Lagan. They were in use in yards since late Victorian and Edwardian times up until the 1960s, when conditions belatedly improved. In these toilets a 'shithouse clerk', as he was dubbed, monitored workers in and out of the toilets.

The toilets were always outside the main workshops and unheated.

Later, in order to 'improve' conditions, enamel then porcelain pans were fitted instead of the hole boards.

One of the pranks played in yards was that the person in the stall adjacent to the flush tank would place a piece of scrunged-up newspaper in the trough just prior to the flush and light it. During its journey down the trough several seated bottoms may well have been singed. The prankster vacated his stall as quickly as he could in order to avoid a thumping!

The late Nicholas Parsons served his engineering apprenticeship during the Second World War at Drysdale's of Yoker on Clydebank, who specialised in pumps and turbines. Little had changed, and his description of the toilets from his Autobiography *My Life in Comedy* is unsurpassed:

There was one building in the middle of the works that was used by everyone on the shop floor. This had been designed with no thought for privacy: just two facing rows of white china toilets with no seats, each separated by a low partition. At the swing-door entrance was an elderly man in a little wooden cubicle with a shelf in front of him, who gave you a metal counter with a number on it, which entitled you to a seven-minute session.

The man's name was Sam, known to everyone, inevitably, as 'S***house Sam'. He ran the place like a boating pond, keeping a close eye on proceedings, regularly announcing: 'Number five, your time is up, come on oot' or, 'Number three, 30 seconds to go.'

He smoked a combination of what was described to me as 'thick black and old shag', which slightly relieved the other pungent odours.

Once you received your metal disc, you knew there was a vacant seat. You had to remember to take a newspaper: toilet paper was unheard of.

You went to the empty pan and joined the nine other men squatting in a row with their boiler suits around their ankles, arms on knees, holding copies of the *Daily Mirror* or *Daily Record*. Opposite was another row of men doing exactly the same.

Hygiene was maintained by an automatic flushing system, which was activated every two minutes, beginning at one end and rushing down the line. It generated a fair amount of power, so if you did not rise at the crucial moment you could get very wet.

Every flush would be heralded by a rumbling in the pipes. It was customary, therefore, for the man nearest the start of the flush, on hearing the warning noise, to shout down the line: 'It's on its way lads. Arses up!'

Ten naked bums would then rise in unison to avoid a soaking. It may have been basic, but you can get used to anything if there is no alternative.

During one of my escapes to relieve my aching back muscles, the gaffer burst in and dragged me away, announcing at the top of his voice that my time was up and that it was also my second visit that day.

It is difficult to maintain any poise with your trousers and boiler suit around your ankles.

A daunting description of the spartan conditions that yard workers had to endure during their 'convenience' time. Naturally, Harland & Wolff's being a much larger yard than Drysdale, the toilet stalls would have been much more numerous.

Those unfortunate workers in the toilets unable to complete their ablutions in the allotted 'convenience' time (probably five minutes back in Edwardian times) were reported to the timekeeper and their wages docked accordingly, mainly by a minimum of thirty minutes. In order to avoid this docking, some workers answered the call of nature close to where they worked; this only added to insanitary conditions.

It is easy to look back on these facilities with humour or perhaps disbelief, but the conditions really were rather basic, bordering on the primitive.

While fitting out afloat it was undesirable, and regarded as time-consuming, for the on-board workforce to go trooping ashore to use the toilet. In order to accommodate this, a temporary toilet was installed. Photos of the *Titanic* during fitting out, show it starboard on the foredeck like a stalactite structure hanging down towards the water. Details of its operation are scant. One can only assume that the effluent discharged directly into the River Lagan.

But to end on a more serious note away from the yard lavatories: to mark the centenary of the Dockers Strike in 1907, a stained-glass window was dedicated in Belfast City Hall on Thursday, 11 May 2007, which reads:

Not as Catholics or Protestants
Not as Nationalists or Unionists
But as Belfast Workers, standing together.

The *Titanic* fitting out. The long appendage from her starboard bow is the on-board workmen's toilets. (Authors' collection)

EPILOGUE

Although the 'Golden' era of this volume has been covered and its scope ceased at the end of the 1920s, the Harland & Wolff yard went on to develop further. In 1934 the White Star Line merged with Cunard, bringing down the curtain on the long association between the two companies.

As mentioned, Workman, Clark & Co. Ltd was re-styled as Norman, Clark in 1928, and in 1936 the company was liquidated and the yard dismantled.

During the Second World War, the yard's workforce swelled to around 31–35,000 to cope with the demand of warship construction.

Between 1945 and 1950, 235 vessels were ordered, 114 ships completed, 25,000 workforce.

In 1961, the *Canberra* (Yard No. 1621) was the last large passenger liner built by Harland & Wolff for the P&O Company.

Harland & Wolff ceased trading on 5 August 2019.

On 19 October 2019, the remnants of the once great shipyard were bought by a London-based energy company, Infra Strata, for £6 million.

From the period covered in this work, the UK and Northern Ireland has largely ceased as a shipbuilding nation. The very nature of the industry has changed over the twentieth century from the labour-intensive industry dominated by riveters and caulkers through to electric arc welding as a method of joining. Casting and forging gave way to welded prefabrication. Instead of ships drawn in offices by cohorts of draughtsmen then being built on exposed slipways, frame and beam style, growing like some massive metal carcass, they are now computer designed and huge modular weldments assembled together in dry docks or halls. All electrical, piping and air-conditioning services are also built in and connected.

The *Ceramic*. In 1934 her ownership passed to Shaw Savill, who had her refurbished by Harland & Wolff in 1936 but she still retained her coal-burning boilers. She was taken up as a troopship in 1940 and later sunk by German submarine U515 on 6/7 December 1942 west of the Azores with only a single survivor. (Authors' collection)

Workman, Clark had a long-standing building programme with Alfred Holt & Co. (Blue Funnel Line). The 14,501grt *Nestor* (Yard No. 318) entered service in 1913. She was taken up as a troopship in the First World War, subsequently resuming commercial service until she was scrapped at Fastlane in July 1950. (Authors' collection)

The main diesel driving units are installed complete into the vessel and not built up as in the past. When ready, instead of gliding down the inclined ways into the sea, the dock in which the vessel has been built is flooded up gently.

Trades were streamlined, apprenticeships shortened and made multidisciplinary, such that an artisan is competent in electrical, mechanical and instrumentation specialisms. Shipyard toilets are now inside the main factories and centrally heated.

Bibby Lines *Oxfordshire* (Yard No. 429), which entered service in September 1912, was taken up for trooping in both world wars. Bibby sold her in 1951 for further trading as a Pakistani pilgrim ship, the *Safini-el-Arab*. She was later scrapped in 1958. Her forty-six years in service were a tribute to Harland & Wolff's engineering skills. (Authors' collection)

The White Star Passenger tender *Nomadic* (Yard No. 422), completed in 1912 to tender the *Olympic* and *Titanic* at Cherbourg. (US Naval Historical & Heritage Centre)

The *Nomadic* (left) and *Traffic* (Yard No. 423) in their First World War livery operating out of Cherbourg while transporting US troops during the First World War. (US Naval Historical & Heritage Centre)

The 5.30 hooter having sounded, this photo shows the sheer mass of humanity of the workforce streaming off the *Olympic*'s gangways and merging in with the shoreside workers, on their way home during May 1911. (Authors' collection)

BIBLIOGRAPHY

Baker III, Elijah, *Introduction to Steel Shipbuilding* (McGraw-Hill, Inc., 1943).

Cameron, Stephen, *Belfast Shipbuilders: A Titanic Tale* (Colourprint, 2011).

de Kerbrech, Richard P., *Down Amongst the Black Gang: The World & Workplace of R.M.S. Titanic's Stokers* (The History Press, 2014).

de Kerbrech, Richard P., *Ships of the White Star Line* (Ian Allan, 2009).

Dougan, David, *The Shipwrights: The History of the Shipconstructors' and Shipwrights' Association, 1882-1963* (Frank Graham, 1975).

Dunn, Laurence, *Famous Liners of the Past: Belfast Built* (Adlard Coles Ltd, 1964).

Green, Rod, *Building the Titanic: The Creation of History's Most Famous Ocean Liner* (Carlton Books, 1996).

Hogg, Robert S., *Naval Architecture and Ship Construction* (The Institute of Marine Engineers, 1956).

Lynch, Dr John, *Forgotten Shipbuilders of Belfast: Workman, Clark* (Friar's Bush Press, 2004).

Mallett, Alan S. & Bell, Andrew M.B., *The Pirrie-Kylsant Motorships 1915–1932* (Mallett & Bell Publications, 1984).

McCluskie, Tom & Sharpe, Michael; Marriott, Leo, *Titanic & Her Sisters Olympic & Britannic* (Parkgate Books Ltd, 1998).

Morrison, Allan, *See You Jimmy!: The Clyde, Its People and Its Patter* (The Vital Spark, 2003).

Newton, R.N., *Practical Construction of Warships* (Longmans Green, 1957).

Parsons, Nicholas, *My Life in Comedy* (Mainstream Publishing, 2014).

Williams, David L. & de Kerbrech, Richard P., *Great Passenger Ships that Never Were: Damned by Destiny Revisited* (The History Press, 2019).

ARTICLES, LECTURE NOTES AND TECHNICAL PAPERS

Crawford, John, *Belfast City, the Port & Harland & Wolff's Shipyard* (Unpublished papers, n.d.).

de Kerbrech, Richard & Williams, David, 'Made in Belfast' (Illustrated Lecture).

Rebbeck, Dr Denis, 'Harland and Wolff's Shipyards & Engine Works, Belfast' (Paper read at Belfast, September 1952).

World Ship Society Shipyard List compiled by Captain John Landels et al.

www.theyard.info

ACKNOWLEDGEMENTS

We would like to extend our gratitude and thanks to the following persons and organisations for their kindness and support in contributing information and illustrations, or in providing other help, without whose assistance this publication would certainly not have come to fruition.

Our thanks to Stephen Cameron and Colourprint for allowing us to use passages from his book *Belfast Built – A Titanic Tale* and his knowledge of shipbuilding in Belfast, and to Penguin Random House for giving us permission to quote a passage from Nicholas Parsons's biography *My Life in Comedy*.

Thanks are also due to Phillip Holmes and David Hutchings, both time-served Portsmouth Dockyard shipwrights by background, and to Mike Milne, a former carpenter and joiner (and sometime works fireman) at Camper & Nicholsons and Vosper-Thornycroft. To Allan Mallett for the use of rare photographs from his collection. In addition, thanks to the late John Crawford of Belfast, Billy Nelson, a former Outfit Manager with Harland & Wolff and Stephen Raffield.

And finally, our thanks to Amy Rigg of The History Press in sharing our vision for this project and taking it up.

Right: A ship starts here. Two men, possibly platers, operating the punching machine. The keel plate, maybe 1-inch thick, is being fed through where a punch pierces out the holes equi-distant apart. The hole blanks are in a pile under the machine. (Authors' collection)

Overleaf: Yard No. 958, the *Sydney Star* on 8 January 1935. Here men are laying the keel on No 12 Slipway in the East Yard immediately after the *Australia Star* had been launched from the same slipway. (Authors' collection)